복습 종이

shimson syntax

심우철 지음

심슨 구문

목차

1

문장 해석법

복습종이

심슨 구문

UNIT 01

전 + 명/명 of 명

🔒 구문분석집 p. 4

→ 〈심순 구문〉 교재 내 수록

[01 - 13] 다음을 해석하세요.

`01` → 구문 패턴 확인하기

01 the baby on the sofa

✏️

02 the development of science

✏️

`01, 02`

03 under the development of science

✏️

`02`

04 an important part of the physical environment

✏️

`02`

05 one of the interesting things

✏️

`02`

06 one of the most destructive forms of all the storms

✏️

01
sofa 소파

02
development 발전

04
physical 물질의, 물리적인
environment 환경

05
interesting 흥미로운

06
destructive 파괴적인

01, 02

07 one of the most common mistakes in reasoning

✎

07
mistake 실수
reasoning 추론

02

08 years of research / lots of students / a kind of sports
hundreds of / millions of students

✎

08
research 연구

01, 02

09 millions of students from several colleges around Dublin

✎

09
college 대학

01, 02

10 over two million acres of land in the country

✎

10
acre 에이커(토지 면적 단위)

01, 02

11 the availability of oxygen in many parts of the sea

✎

11
availability 이용도
oxygen 산소

01, 02

12 the poor performance of American students on various international
tests

✎

12
performance 수행, 성취
various 다양한
international 국제적인

01, 02

13 one of the fundamental rights of every human being without
distinction of race

✎

13
fundamental 기초의, 기본의
distinction 구분, 구별, 차이

UNIT 02

A, (B,) and C/형 + 명

🔒 구문분석집 p. 6

[01 - 15] 다음을 해석하세요.

`04`
01 a very beautiful girl

01
beautiful 아름다운

`04`
02 with a very beautiful girl

`03, 04`
03 the powers of imagination and inner visualization

03
imagination 상상(력)
inner 내부의
visualization 심상

`03`
04 books, movies, software, and pictures

04
software 소프트웨어

`03, 04`
05 the creator or author of books, movies, software, and pictures

05
creator 창작자

`03, 04`
06 the earliest and most effective machines available to humans

06
effective 효과적인
machine 기계
available 이용할 수 있는

`03, 04`
07 one of the most famous yet mysterious celebrities of recent times

07
mysterious 신비한
celebrity 유명인
recent 최근의

`03, 04`
08 15 years of research on U.S. employment and the minimum wage

08
employment 고용
minimum 최소
wage 임금

09 his absolutely outstanding performance in an exceptionally difficult condition

✎

10 the important value of life such as honesty, good manners, team work, and cooperation

✎

11 three rows of benches on each side of the stage and six rows in front of the principal

✎

12 the development of new types of products and services and new forms and methods of distribution

✎

13 I bought a very expensive car.

✎

14 I bought a very expensive car from the car-dealer's shop 5 years ago.

✎

15 I bought a very expensive car with leather seats, a comfortable house, and costly gems.

✎

09
absolutely 절대적으로
outstanding 현저한
exceptionally 유난히, 특별히

10
value 가치
such as ~와 같은
honesty 정직
manner 태도
cooperation 협동

11
row 줄, 열
principal 교장

12
product 생산품, 제품
method 방법
distribution 분배, 배분

13
expensive 비싼

14
car-dealer 자동차 판매업자

15
leather 가죽
comfortable 편안한
costly 값이 비싼
gem 보석

PART 1

문장 해석법

준동사는 하나의 구

🔒 구문분석집 p. 8

[01 - 08] 다음을 해석하세요.

`05`

01 to read important materials in either quiet or noisy rooms

✏️

01
material 자료
quiet 조용한
noisy 시끄러운

`05`

02 the best way to get data from healthy male volunteers

✏️

02
data 데이터
healthy 건강한
male 남성의
volunteer 지원자

`05`

03 the necessity to make a good first impression

✏️

03
necessity 필요(성)
impression 인상

`06`

04 examining scientific research on climate change

✏️

04
examine 시험하다
scientific 과학적인
climate 기후

`06`

05 the excitement of leaving for a foreign country

✏️

05
excitement 흥분
foreign 외국의

`06`

06 the books containing valuable insights on leadership

✏️

06
contain 담고 있다
valuable 귀중한
insight 통찰(력)

07

07 Trying to communicate in another person's language is essential to building strong relationships across diverse cultures and backgrounds.

communicate 의사소통하다
essential 필수의
relationship 관계
diverse 다양한

🖊

05, 06

08

08 The failure to communicate our feelings effectively can lead to misunderstanding and strain in relationships with others.

failure 실패
effectively 효과적으로
lead to ~으로 이어지다
misunderstanding 오해
strain 긴장

🖊

동사란?

🔒 구문분석집 p. 10

[01 - 18] 다음을 해석하세요.

08

01   Today many Native Americans are fighting their problems.
✏️

01
Native Americans 아메리카 원주민
fight 싸우다

09

02   On the other hand, the water for the fields is taken from a number of small ponds or streams.
✏️

02
on the other hand 반면에
pond 못
stream 시내, 개울

10

03   The TV programs have not affected all of us in an identical way.
✏️

03
affect ~에 영향을 주다
identical 동일한

09, 10

04   Under the development of science, the lifespan of human has been lengthened.
✏️

04
lifespan 수명
lengthen 늘이다

09, 10

05   Over the years, various systems of grading coins have been developed by antique coin specialists.
✏️

05
grade 등급을 매기다
coin 동전
antique 골동품의
specialist 전문가

09, 12

06   Elements of culture can be divided into two categories.
✏️

06
element 요소
culture 문화
divide 나누다
category 범주, 카테고리

07 Peter had never been on a blind date before, so he was very nervous when he first dated Jane.

9, 11

07
blind date 소개팅

---

08 The cities themselves cannot be developed without the prior development of the rural areas.

09, 12

08
prior 앞선
rural 시골의, 지방의

---

09 During her lifetime, she may really have felt like a nobody, for few people knew her outside of her small hometown.

13

09
lifetime 일생, 생애
hometown 고향

---

10 Mike's on a business trip, so he can't have been at the meeting.

13

10
business trip 출장

---

11 You cannot have felt the earthquake, for it was so slight.

13

11
earthquake 지진
slight 약간의

---

12 The accident must have taken place on the crosswalk.

13

12
accident 사고
crosswalk 횡단보도

---

13 Kelly should have taken the medicine after her meal, not before.

13

13
medicine 약
meal 식사

12, 13

14 The radio, the movie, and the airplane should have taught us that technology may be beneficent but may also serve evil purpose.

✎

14
technology 기술
beneficent 유익한
serve 이바지하다, 도움이 되다
evil 나쁜, 사악한
purpose 목적

12, 14

15 Agriculture will continue to develop in three main ways.

✎

15
agriculture 농업
continue 계속하다, 지속하다

12, 14

16 You might first want to read something about how the engine operates.

✎

16
engine 엔진
operate 작동하다, 움직이다

09, 14

17 By the year 2030, the area of the earth's forests is expected to diminish by a fifth.

✎

17
area 지역
forest 숲
expect 예정되어 있다
diminish 감소하다

15

18 The appreciation of art results in a happier feeling and deeper understanding of other people and the world.

✎

18
appreciation 감상, 평가
result in (결과적으로) ~을 낳다[야기하다]

동사를 잡는 법

🔒 구문분석집 p. 13

[01 - 26] 다음을 해석하세요.

01
Last year, more than half of the box-office revenues of Japan's movie industry came from animations.

🖉

01
half 반, 절반
revenue 수익, 이익
industry 산업
animation 애니메이션

02
One of the most remarkable things about the human mind is our ability to imagine the future.

🖉

02
remarkable 주목할 만한
ability 능력
imagine 상상하다

03
One of the advantages of technology is its ability to facilitate communication and connect people from around the world.

🖉

03
advantage 유리, 이익
facilitate 촉진하다, 쉽게 하다
connect 연결하다

04
Indeed, the amount of information available to children is quickening the beginning of adulthood.

🖉

04
indeed 실로, 참으로
amount 양
information 정보
available 이용할 수 있는
quicken 빠르게 하다
adulthood 성인

05
Hundreds of statues of Greek and Roman gods such as Apollo, Jupiter, and Neptune stood in the gardens.

🖉

05
statue 조각상
god 신
garden 정원

06 [17]

The reason for the ubiquitous production of light by the microorganisms of the sea remains obscure.

🖉

06	
reason 이유	
ubiquitous 곳곳에 있는	
production 생산	
light 빛, 광선	
microorganism 미생물	
remain 남아 있다	
obscure 분명치 않은	

07 [16]

The outstanding achievements of African-Americans have been stolen or overlooked, despite their great significance.

🖉

07
achievement 성취, 달성
steal 훔치다, 몰래 빼앗다
overlook 못 보고 넘어가다
despite ~에도 불구하고
significance 의미

08 [16]

The rates of gun homicide and other gun crimes in the United States have dropped since highs in the early 1990's.

🖉

08
rate 비율
homicide 살인
crime 범죄
drop 떨어지다

09 [20]

Many people consider her the most influential social science researcher of the twentieth century.

🖉

09
consider ~으로 생각하다
influential 영향을 미치는

10 [20]

A number of gun advocates consider ownership a birthright and an essential part of the nation's heritage.

🖉

10
a number of 많은
advocate 옹호하다, 변호하다
ownership 소유권
birthright 생득권
essential 근본적인, 필수의
heritage 유산

11 [16]

By some estimates, deforestation has resulted in the loss of as much as eighty percent of the natural forests of the world.

🖉

11
estimate 평가, 견적
deforestation 삼림 벌채
result in (그 결과) ~ 되다
loss 손실, 손해

12 Coffee with bitter and slightly acidic flavor has a stimulating effect on humans, primarily due to its caffeine content.

✎

12
bitter 쓴
slightly 약간, 조금
acidic 매우 신, 산성의
stimulating 자극적인
effect 효과
primarily 원래, 주로
due to ~ 때문에
caffeine 카페인
content 함유(량), 내용물

13 Some Australian aborigines can keep changing their name throughout their life as the result of some important experience.

✎

13
aborigine 원주민
throughout ~을 통하여
experience 경험

14 Would we, however, prefer to fill the developing minds of our children with hundreds of geometry problems or the names of all the rivers in the world?

✎

14
prefer ~을 좋아하다
fill 채우다
develop 발전하다
mind 마음, 정신
geometry 기하학

15 Facilities in the rural areas, such as transport, health, and education services, should be improved to foster a more positive attitude to rural life.

✎

15
facility 시설, 설비
transport 수송, 운송
education 교육
foster 육성하다, 촉진하다
positive 긍정적인
attitude 태도

16 Rapid progress in global free trade under the World Trade Organization virtually removes national boundaries in the flow of money and commodities.

✎

16
rapid 빠른
progress 진보, 발달
global 지구의, 전 세계의
trade 무역
World Trade Organization
세계무역기구(WTO)
virtually 사실상
remove 제거하다
boundary 경계(선)
flow 흐름
commodity 상품, 일용품

PART 1

문장 해석법

17 The flexible mind of the men in both countries makes the difference between the position of women in Korea and that of women in the United States.

✏️

18 The most widely adopted conceptualization of burnout has been developed by Maslach and her colleagues in their studies of human service workers.

✏️

19 Institutions such as Indiana University Bloomington offer automatic awards to high-performing students with good GPAs and class ranks.

✏️

20 Some companies offered all students online teaching alternatives instead of classroom teaching due to the risk of infection of the coronavirus.

✏️

21 A hamburger and French fries became the typical American meal in the 1950s, thanks to the promotional efforts of the fast food chains.

✏️

17
flexible 유연한, 융통성이 있는
difference 차이
position 위치, 입장

18
widely 널리
adopt 채택하다
conceptualization 개념화
burnout (심신의) 소모
colleague 동료

19
institution 기관
offer 제공하다
automatic 자동적으로 따라오는, 자동의
award 상, 상금
high-performing 성취도가 높은
GPA(grade point average) 평점
rank 순위, 등급

20
company 회사
alternative 대안
instead of ~ 대신
risk 위험성
infection 감염, 전염
coronavirus 코로나바이러스

21
typical 전형적인, 대표적인
thanks to ~ 덕분에, 때문에
promotional 홍보의
effort 노력, 수고
chain 가맹점

16

22 However, elevated levels and/or long-term exposure to air pollution can lead to more serious symptoms and conditions affecting human health.

22
elevate 올리다, 높이다
level 수준
long-term 장기의
exposure 노출
pollution 오염, 공해
serious 심각한
symptom 증상
condition 상태
affect ~에게 영향을 주다

17

23 The decline in the number of domestic adoptions in developed countries is mainly the result of a falling supply of domestically adoptable children.

23
decline 쇠퇴, 감소
domestic 국내의
adoption 입양
developed country 선진국
mainly 주로
falling 하락하는, 떨어지는
supply 공급
domestically 국내에서
adoptable 양자로 삼을 수 있는

17

24 The pleasures of contact with the natural world are available to anyone who will place himself under the influence of a lonely mountain top or the stillness of a forest.

24
pleasure 기쁨, 즐거움
contact 접촉
influence 영향(력)
lonely 외로운
stillness 고요

18

25 Workers in manufacturing jobs are likely to suffer serious health problems as a result of the noise, or the stress of being paced by mechanical requirements of the assembly line.

25
manufacturing 제조업의
be likely to ~할 것 같다
suffer 경험하다, 겪다
noise 소음
pace 속도를 조정하다
mechanical 기계의
requirement 필요조건
assembly line 조립 라인

18

26 We need to spend less time teaching children what to learn, and more time teaching children how to learn.

26
spend (돈·노력·시간 등을) 쓰다, 들이다

🔒 구문분석집 p. 19

[01 - 11] 다음을 해석하세요.

`21`

01   The movie convinced me that I had still loved him.

01

convince ~에게 깨닫게 하다
still 여전히

`21`

02   The doctor informed her that her baby had a special disease.

02

inform ~에게 알리다
disease 질병

`21`

03   I promise you that the same quality of service will be maintained irrespective of external factors.

03

promise 약속하다
quality 질, 품질
maintain 지속하다, 유지하다
irrespective 관계없는
external 외부의
factor 요인, 요소

`21`

04   The boss asked me if the project could be completed by next week's deadline.

04

boss 상관, 상사
project 계획, 과제
complete 완성하다, 달성하다
deadline 마감 (기한)

`21`

05   The teacher told the students what they needed to study for the upcoming exam.

05

upcoming 다가오는
exam 시험

06 The presentation showed investors when the market conditions would be most favorable.

06
presentation 발표
investor 투자자
favorable 유리한, 형편이 좋은

07 The teacher showed the students when to apply the grammar rules in writing essays.

07
apply 적용하다
grammar 문법
rule 규칙
essay 과제물, 짧은 글

08 The accident in 1986 at Chernobyl reminded the world that it is very important to use nuclear power responsibly.

08
accident 사고, 사건
remind ~에게 깨닫게 하다
important 중요한
nuclear power 원자력
responsibly 책임감 있게

09 Governments should continuously remind themselves that medium-term recovery efforts can stop droughts from turning into famines.

09
government 정부
continuously 잇달아, 연속으로
medium-term 중단기적인
recovery 회복, 복구
drought 가뭄
turn into ~으로 변하다
famine 기근, 식량 부족

10 The professor showed the class, through practical examples and case studies, how economic theories apply in real-world scenarios.

10
professor 교수
practical 실제의, 실용적인
example 예, 보기
case study 사례
economic 경제의
theory 이론
real-world 현실에 존재하는
scenario 시나리오, 각본

11 After a progressive program to teach the kids to wash their hands properly several times during the day, their understanding of the importance of hand-washing has increased.

11
progressive 점진적인
properly 적당하게, 알맞게
understanding 이해
importance 중요
increase 증가하다

PART 1

문장 해석법

UNIT 07

지각동사/사역동사/준사역동사

🔒 구문분석집 p. 21

[01 - 15] 다음을 해석하세요.

`22`

01 I watched a man on the Metro try to get off the train and fail.

🖉

01
get off (차에서) 내리다
fail 실패하다

`22`

02 He heard the news anchor report the latest updates on the situation.

🖉

02
anchor (뉴스) 사회자, 진행자
update 업데이트, 최신 정보
situation 상황

`22`

03 He saw the old bridge rebuilt with sturdy materials by the construction workers.

🖉

03
rebuild 재건하다
sturdy 튼튼한, 억센
material 재료, 자재
construction 건설

`23`

04 The teacher made her students finish their homework before leaving the classroom.

🖉

04
homework 숙제
classroom 교실

`23`

05 The school had its playground renovated for the students' safety.

🖉

05
playground 운동장
renovate 개선하다
safety 안전

`23`

06 I can't make myself understood in English.
　cf His explanation made me understand what he had said before.

🖉

06
understand 이해하다
explanation 설명

07

`24`

07 He helped me move all the furniture into my new apartment.

✏️

furniture 가구

08

`24`

08 I need to get my project finished by the end of this week.

✏️

finish 끝내다, 마치다
week 주

09

`24`

09 Many people got us to participate in the community cleanup event last Saturday morning.

✏️

participate in ~에 참가하다
community 지역사회
cleanup 대청소
event 행사

10

`24`

10 Reading stories and poetry, for instance, can help us understand and improve our own situations.

✏️

poetry 시
for instance 예를 들어
improve 개선하다
situation 상황, 사정

11

`23`

11 Even if the efforts to make the world around you change do not come true, don't be frustrated.

✏️

come true 실현되다
frustrated 실망한, 좌절된

12

`22`

12 Many coaches have often seen highly talented young athletes fail in their performances due to a lack of mental abilities.

✏️

highly 대단히
talented 재능 있는
athlete 운동선수
fail 실패하다
performance 성취, 수행
lack 부족, 결핍
mental 정신의, 심적인

13

`22`

13 People should not hesitate to contact the police if they've noticed anyone acting suspiciously.

✏️

hesitate 주저하다, 망설이다
contact 연락하다
notice ~을 인지하다
suspiciously 의심스럽게

14 In a survey published earlier this year, seven out of ten parents said that they would never let their children play with toy guns.

survey 설문조사
publish 발표하다
toy gun 장난감 총

15 Tory Higgins and his colleagues had university students read a personality description of someone and then summarize it for someone else who was believed either to like or to dislike this person.

personality 개성, 성격
description 기술, 묘사
summarize 요약하다
dislike 싫어하다

UNIT

08

COREAFP 동사

🔒 구문분석집 p. 24

[01 - 12] 다음을 해석하세요.

`25`

01 The poor harvest caused prices to rise sharply.

🖉

01
harvest 수확(량)
rise 오르다, 상승하다
sharply 급격하게

`25`

02 All assignments are expected to be turned in on time.

🖉

02
assignment 과제
turn in 제출하다
on time 제때에

`25`

03 Rainy season forced the travelers to spend most of the vacation indoors.

🖉

03
rainy season 장마철
indoors 실내에서

`25`

04 Unexpectedly poor sales have forced the company to postpone planned wage increases indefinitely.

🖉

04
unexpectedly 예상외로, 갑자기
postpone 연기하다, 미루다
planned 계획된, 예정된
wage 임금
indefinitely 무기한으로

`25`

05 Team members are being asked to postpone any vacations until the entire project has been completed.

🖉

05
entire 전체의, 전부의
complete 완료하다

`25`

06 A vacation policy allowing employees to take unlimited time off sounds unreasonable for any company.

🖉

06
policy 정책, 방침
employee 직원
take time off 휴가를 내다
unlimited 한없는
unreasonable 비합리적인

07 [25]

To encourage people to stay in rural areas, the government should provide more comfortable facilities such as health and education services.

✎

08 [25]

All airlines in Brazil currently permit all passengers to check in two pieces of baggage on international flights to and from the country.

✎

09 [25]

The uncertain economic condition of recent years has caused union and management representatives to explore many ways of handling labor problems.

✎

10 [25]

An increased awareness of the effects of plastic bags has caused many states and countries to implement plastic bag-related legislation.

✎

11 [25]

This telecom company has been a global pioneer of mobile phone banking, enabling people to transfer money with a minimum of fuss.

✎

12 [25]

Small farmers have actually been compelled to switch to organic production because they cannot afford chemical fertilizers.

✎

07
stay 머무르다, 남다
provide 주다, 공급하다

08
airline 항공사
currently 현재
permit 허가하다
passenger 승객
check in 투숙하다, 짐을 부치다
baggage 수화물
international 국제적인
flight 항공편

09
uncertain 불확실한
economic 경제의
recent 최근의
union and management 노사
representative 대표자, 대리인
explore 탐구하다, 조사하다
handle 취급하다, 처리하다
labor 노동, 근로

10
awareness 인식, 지각
effect 효과, 영향
plastic bag 비닐봉지
implement 이행[실행]하다
legislation 법률, 법령

11
telecom(=telecommunication)
원거리 통신
pioneer 개척자
enable 가능하게 하다
transfer 이동하다
minimum 최소, 최저
fuss 소란, 야단, 불편

12
switch 바꾸다, 전환하다
organic 유기의
afford ~의 여유가 있다
chemical fertilizer 화학비료

분리·박탈/인지/제공/금지·억제 동사

🔒 구문분석집 p. 26

[01 - 12] 다음을 해석하세요.

01 Adults have deprived a lot of children of a normal home life.

01
adult 성인, 어른
normal 정상의, 보통의

02 Because society has deprived women of many equal rights, feminists have fought for equality.

02
society 사회
equal 같은, 동등한
right 권리
feminist 페미니스트
equality 평등

03 The cyber-attack stripped the company of sensitive data and confidential information.

03
cyber-attack 사이버 공격
sensitive 민감한
confidential 기밀의
information 정보

04 The dictator's oppressive regime stripped the people in the society of their basic human rights and freedoms.

04
dictator 독재자
oppressive 억압적인
regime 정권, 체제
freedom 자유

05 The lecture provided him with an opportunity to meet one of his heroes.

05
lecture 강의, 강연
opportunity 기회
hero 영웅, 위인

06 The Korean government presented coach Guus Hiddink with honorary citizenship and a passport.

06
honorary 명예의
citizenship 시민권
passport 여권

07
28

An informer supplied the police with the names of those involved in the crime.

✎

29
08

The teacher kept the students from talking during the exam to maintain a quiet testing environment.

✎

29
09

The company policy prohibits employees from accessing certain websites during work hours.

✎

29
10

Ignorance and superstition about law and legal process prevent some members from benefiting from a modern civil system of justice.

✎

27
11

The smell of freshly baked cakes always reminds me of my grandmother's kitchen.

✎

27
12

Another effective way to track and notify customers of their e-commerce orders is to use email and SMS notifications.

✎

07
informer 정보원
police 경찰
involve 관련[연루]시키다
crime (범)죄

08
maintain 지속하다, 유지하다
quiet 조용한, 고요한
testing 시험
environment 환경

09
access 접속하다, 접근하다
certain 특정한

10
ignorance 무지
superstition 미신
law 법률, 법
legal 법률의
process 절차, 과정
benefit (~에서) 득을 보다
modern 현대의
civil 민사의, 시민의
system of justice 사법제도

11
freshly 새로이
bake (빵 등을) 굽다

12
effective 효과적인
track 추적하다
customer 손님
e-commerce 전자 상거래
notification 알림, 통지

MEMO

2

절 해석법

복습종이

심슨 구문

🔒 구문분석집 p. 30

[01 - 13] 다음을 해석하세요.

30

01 One of his major achievements was rebuilding Kyongbok Palace which was burnt down during the Japanese invasion in 1592.

✏️

30

02 The company now hears from roughly 10 couples a day who met online and are now planning a wedding.

✏️

30

03 The movie, which I watched last weekend, had an unexpected plot twist that kept me on the edge of my seat.

✏️

30

04 To keep out evil spirits, they hang a rope of straw which stands for happiness and good luck, across the front of their houses.

✏️

30

05 There are many organizations whose sole purpose is to help mentally retarded children.

✏️

01
major 주요한, 중요한
achievement 업적, 공로
rebuild 재건하다, 다시 짓다
burn down 전소하다
invasion 침입, 침략

02
hear from ~로부터 연락을 받다[소식을 듣다]
roughly 대충, 대략
wedding 결혼식

03
unexpected 예기치 못한, 의외의
plot 줄거리, 플롯
twist 예상 밖의 전개, 반전
on the edge of one's seat (영화·이야기 등에) 매료되어

04
keep out 못 들어오게 하다
evil spirit 악령, 악귀
hang 매달다, 걸다
rope 밧줄, 끈
straw 짚
stand for ~을 나타내다, 상징하다

05
organization 기관, 조직
sole 유일한
purpose 목적
mentally retarded 지적장애의

06 From time to time we must look up words whose meanings we do not know.

✎

07 I approached the tree in which many soldiers had been hanged in the war.

✎

08 This wind has traveled from the North Pole toward which I am going.

✎

09 I have two favorite hobbies: painting and gardening, both of which allow me to express my creativity and connect with nature in meaningful ways.

✎

10 Similarly, corn in Latin America is traditionally ground or soaked with limestone, which makes available a B vitamin in the corn, the absence of which would otherwise lead to a deficiency disease.

✎

11 Not knowing what to do, I climbed up to the top of a tall tree, from which I looked around to see if I could discover anything that could give me hope.

✎

06
look up 찾아보다
word 단어

07
approach ~에 가까이 다가가다
soldier 군인
hang 목 매달다
war 전쟁

08
travel 이동하다
North Pole 북극

09
favorite 좋아하는
hobby 취미
gardening 정원 가꾸기, 원예
express 표현하다
creativity 창의성
connect with ~과 연결하다
meaningful 의미 있는

10
similarly 비슷하게, 마찬가지로
traditionally 전통적으로
grind 갈다, 빻다
soak 스며들다
limestone 석회석
available 이용할 수 있는
absence 없음, 결핍
otherwise 그렇지 않으면
lead to ~로 이어지다
deficiency disease 결핍증

11
discover 발견하다
hope 희망

12 The concept of this connection between smell and health has created a huge aroma therapy industry, which puts scented oils into everything from shaving cream to candles, from shampoo to lipstick.

✎

12
concept 개념, 생각
connection 연결, 관계
create 창조하다
huge 거대한, 막대한
industry 산업
scented 향기가 나는
oil 기름
shaving cream 면도용 크림
candle 양초

13 In fact, the movie business and the athletic world are full of intelligent, educated, and informed men and women who are interested and involved in a wide variety of activities and causes.

✎

13
in fact 실제, 사실은
athletic 운동의, 체육의
intelligent 지적인
educated 교양 있는
informed 견문이 넓은
a wide variety of 매우 다양한
cause 대의명분

관계부사

🔒 구문분석집 p. 33

[01 - 06] 다음을 해석하세요.

`32`

01 They lived near the shore where there were many shells.

✏️

01
shore 바닷가, 해안
shell 조개

`32`

02 There are two very short periods each year when climbing is possible.

✏️

02
period 기간
climbing 등산
possible 가능한, 할 수 있는

`32`

03 We managed to find a couple of benches where we thought we could spend the rest of the night.

✏️

03
manage to ~하다[해내다]
find 찾아내다, 발견하다
a couple of 두서너 개의
bench 벤치
spend 보내다, 지내다
rest 나머지

`32`

04 Clearly, modern societies are facing a major change into a new economic system where human resourcefulness counts far more than natural resources.

✏️

04
clearly 확실히
face ~에 직면하다
resourcefulness 자원이 많음
count 중요하다
natural resources 천연자원

`32`

05 I still remember the awesome feeling I had on that day in May when my little feet carried me up the stairs into the grandstands at the car racing stadium.

✏️

05
remember 기억하다
awesome 엄청난, 멋진
carry 이끌다
stair 계단
grandstand 관람석
stadium 경기장, 스타디움

06 Climate change has narrowed the range where bumblebees are found in North America and Europe in recent decades, according to a recent study, published in the journal *Science*.

06
narrow 좁히다
range 범위, 한계
bumblebee 호박벌
decade 10년(간)
according to ~에 의하면
publish 발표하다

UNIT 12 의문사

🔒 구문분석집 p. 34

[01 - 20] 다음을 해석하세요.

33

01 What will the future of transportation look like with the rise of electric vehicles?

🖊

01
future 미래
transportation 운송, 수송
rise 증가, 상승
electric vehicle 전기차

33

02 What effects does climate change have on global weather patterns and ecosystems?

🖊

02
effect 효과, 영향
climate change 기후 변화
global 지구의, 전 세계의
weather 날씨, 기후
ecosystem 생태계

34

03 How will artificial intelligence influence the environment?

🖊

03
artificial intelligence 인공지능
influence ~에 영향을 미치다

33

04 Have you decided which one you're going to buy?

🖊

04
decide 결정하다

33

05 I want to know who will be appointed the FIFA referees for this year.

🖊

05
appoint 임명하다
referee 심판

33

06 This match will show who the best player in the world is.

🖊

06
match 경기, 시합
show 보여 주다, 제시하다

33

07 The man asked her what kind of things she did in her spare time.

🖊

07
spare time 여가 시간

PART 2

절 해석법

08

`34`

08 There are many theories about why the dinosaurs went extinct.

✎

08
theory 이론
dinosaur 공룡
extinct 멸종한

`34`

09 Mary wondered where her son lost his wristwatch.

✎

09
wonder 궁금하다
lose 잃어버리다
wristwatch 손목시계

`33`

10 Who we are is reflected in what we won't eat as well as what we will.

✎

10
reflect 반영하다, 나타내다
B as well as A A뿐 아니라 B도 역시

`34`

11 Nobody could understand where we ever got money enough to keep us with food in our bellies.

✎

11
belly 배, 복부

`33`

12 It's a good idea to consider what short-term goals we can accomplish.

✎

12
consider 숙고하다, 검토하다
short-term 단기의
goal 목표
accomplish 이루다, 달성하다

`34`

13 She demonstrated to us how surprisingly effective the new study method was for improving memory retention.

✎

13
demonstrate 증명하다, 입증하다
surprisingly 놀랍게도
effective 효과적인
method 방법
improve 개선하다
memory 기억(력)
retention 보존, 유지

`34`

14 The scientist explained to the students how she discovered how to extract the compound from the plant.

✎

14
explain 설명하다
discover 발견하다
extract 추출하다
compound 합성물, 화합물
plant 식물

15 34
The teacher taught his students how they should improve their writing skills through incessant practice and feedback.

16 33
What we will do during our trip to the countryside depends on the weather and the interests of the group.

17 34
How he overcame his fear of public speaking and delivered such a confident presentation impressed everyone in the room.

18 33, 34
We wanted to know what kinds of girls her sisters were, what her father was like, and how long her mother had been dead.

19 33
Scientists have researched what conditions are like beyond the Earth's atmosphere, and what effects space travel has on the human body.

20 34
One way to tell how much sleep you need is to try, for a while, getting to bed in time to wake up without an alarm clock. If you can do it, and if you don't doze off during the day, you've gone to bed at the right time.

15
improve 개선하다
skill 기술, 숙련, 솜씨
incessant 끊임없는
practice 연습
feedback 피드백

16
countryside 시골
depend on ~에 달려 있다
interest 관심

17
overcome 극복하다, 이겨내다
fear 공포, 두려움
public speaking 연설
deliver (연설·강연 등을) 하다
confident 자신감 있는
presentation 발표
impress 깊은 인상을 주다

18
dead 죽은

19
atmosphere 대기
space travel 우주여행

20
in time 일찍
wake up (잠에서) 깨다
alarm clock 자명종
doze off 졸다

UNIT 13

복합관계사

 구문분석집 p. 38

[01 - 10] 다음을 해석하세요.

35

01 Whichever they choose, we must accept their decision.

01
choose 고르다, 선택하다
accept 수락하다
decision 결심, 결정

35

02 Whoever arrives first will be responsible for unlocking the door and turning on the lights.

02
arrive 도착하다
be responsible for ~에 책임이 있다
unlock (열쇠로) 열다
turn on 켜다

35

03 Whichever team wins the championship will earn a trophy and recognition for its hard work.

03
win 이기다
championship 선수권, 우승
earn 얻다, 획득하다
trophy 트로피, 전리품
recognition 인정, 인식, 승인

36

04 However tired you may be, you must do it today.

36

05 However much money you have, you may not be happy.

36

06 Whenever you catch yourself having a fit of worry, stop and change your thoughts.

06
catch 발견하다
fit 욱하는 감정

07 Whatever book you choose from the library has the potential to transport you to different worlds through its captivating storytelling.

07
library 도서관
potential 잠재력; 잠재적인
transport 이동시키다
captivating 매혹적인, 마음을 사로잡는
storytelling 이야기하기

08 He was thought of as the most flattering man in our company, since he accepted whatever his superiors suggested without reflective thinking.

08
flattering 아첨하는
superior 상급자
suggest 제안하다
reflective 숙고하는

09 Your GPS receiver can tell you your exact location and give you directions wherever you need to go, no matter where you are on the planet!

09
receiver 수신기
exact 정확한
location 장소, 위치
direction 방향
the planet 지구

10 No matter how upset you are, keep the feedback job-related and never criticize someone personally because of an inappropriate action.

10
upset 화난, 속상한
job-related 직업[업무]과 관련된
criticize 비평하다, 비난하다
personally 개인적으로
inappropriate 부적절한

PART 2

겹 왜석말

문장 중간에 that

🔒 구문분석집 p. 40

[01 - 12] 다음을 해석하세요.

38
01 Some people feel that their national soccer team represents their country's honor.

🖉

01
represent 상징하다, 대표하다
honor 명예

39
02 There are more than a thousand radio stations that play country music 24 hours a day.

🖉

02
radio station 라디오 방송국

39
03 I agree to the idea that good behavior must be reinforced with incentives.

🖉

03
behavior 행동, 행실
reinforce 강화하다, 보강하다
incentive 인센티브, 격려금

38
04 You gradually become aware that you are a unique person with your own ideas and attitudes.

🖉

04
gradually 점차, 서서히
aware 깨달은, 알고 있는
unique 독특한, 유일한
attitude 태도, 마음가짐

38
05 Advocates of homeschooling believe that children learn better when they are in a secure, loving environment.

🖉

05
advocate 지지자, 변호사
homeschooling 홈스쿨링
secure 안전한
loving 애정 있는
environment 환경

39
06 The program that offers free tutoring sessions to underprivileged children has made a significant impact on their academic performance.

🖉

06
offer 제공하다
free 무료의
tutor 과외를 하다
session 수업
underprivileged 소외계층의
significant 상당한
impact 영향
academic performance 학업 성적

39

07 Researchers have developed a new model that they say will provide better estimates of the North Atlantic right whale population.

✎

07
researcher 연구자
estimate 추정치, 견적

39

08 The news that a cure for a rare disease had been discovered brought hope to countless families affected by the illness.

✎

08
cure 치료(법)
rare disease 희귀질환, 희소 질병
discover 발견하다
countless 수많은
affect ~을 감염시키다
illness 병

38

09 Foreign language associations in the United States say that learning Spanish, French, German, or other languages benefits both elementary and secondary school students.

✎

09
foreign language 외국어
association 협회, 연합
benefit 도움이 되다
elementary 초등교육의
secondary 중등교육의

39

10 In the ancient practice of sending messages through a bearer, people would write secret messages in a substance that would only be revealed on plain paper through the use of a reagent.

✎

10
ancient 고대의, 옛날의
bearer 전달자
secret 비밀의
substance 물질
reveal 드러내다, 알리다
plain paper 백지
reagent 시약, 반응물

38, 39

11 This means that a human law is a set of rules that are valid only for a certain number of people over a certain period of time.

✎

11
law 법
valid 유효한
period 기간

38

12 Studies suggest that when a healthy trust is formed from the start of life, it leads one to moral, honest, balanced conduct in relations with others.

✎

12
healthy 건강한
trust 신뢰, 신용
form 형성하다
moral 도덕적인
balanced 균형이 잡힌
conduct 행동, 행위
relation 관계

🔒 구문분석집 p. 42

UNIT 15

문장 중간에 S + V

[01 - 09] 다음을 해석하세요.

`40`

01 I believed she was still alive.

✎

01
alive 살아 있는

`41`

02 The scientist well documented the findings she discovered during her research project.

✎

02
document (상세한 내용을) 기록하다
finding (조사·연구 등의) 결과, 결론
discover 발견하다

`41`

03 The only difference among societies is the way these events are celebrated.

✎

03
difference 차이점
society 사회
celebrate 기념하다, 축하하다

`40`

04 I believe natural beauty has a necessary place in the spiritual development of any individual or any society.

✎

04
beauty 아름다움
necessary 필요한
spiritual 정신의, 정신적인
development 발전, 발달
individual 개인

`41`

05 Our fascination with science fiction reflected a deep faith technology would lead us to a cyber utopia, with robot servants serving food.

✎

05
fascination 매혹
science fiction 공상 과학 소설
reflect 반영하다
faith 믿음, 신념
utopia 유토피아, 이상국
servant 하인

40

06 Steve's good record at work proved he could handle the job, but his inner voice told him he would fail.

✎

06

record 실적, 기록
prove 증명하다, 입증하다
handle 처리하다, 다루다
inner 내면의, 내부의
fail 실패하다, 실수하다

40

07 An officer of the IMF said the troubled economies would recover from the present economic hardships by the second half of 1999.

✎

07

officer (정부 기관이나 큰 조직체의) 관계자
troubled 어려운, 힘든
economy 경제
recover 회복하다
economic 경제의
hardship 어려움, 곤란

41

08 Do you have a little brother or sister who listens to commercials on television and then tries to get your mother to buy every product he or she has seen advertised?

✎

08

commercial 광고
advertise 광고하다

40

09 The study showed the ability of students to retain knowledge about words improved after one night's sleep even if the students lost some of that knowledge during the day.

✎

09

retain 유지하다, 보유하다
knowledge 지식
improve 향상되다, 개선시키다

S + 관계대명사/관계부사

🔒 구문분석집 p. 44

[01 - 11] 다음을 해석하세요.

42

01 A person who stands up straight conveys a message of energy and self-confidence.

✏️

01
stand up 서 있다
straight 똑바로, 곧게
convey 전달하다, 운반하다
self-confidence 자신감

43

02 The song which I listened to on the radio reminded me of happy memories from my childhood.

✏️

02
remind A of B A에게 B가 생각나게 하다
childhood 어린 시절

42

03 The major reason why spelling in English is difficult is that modern English spelling shows old English pronunciation.

✏️

03
major 주요한, 중요한
reason 이유
spelling 철자(법)
pronunciation 발음

42

04 The park where my family likes to go for walks is filled with beautiful flowers and tall trees.

✏️

04
be filled with ~로 가득 차다

43

05 Our beliefs and the languages we speak are also part of our nonmaterial culture.

✏️

05
belief 신념, 확신
nonmaterial 비물질적인
culture 문화

06 The cost of merchandise you purchased from us several months ago was only $250.

✎

43

06
merchandise 상품
purchase 구입하다, 사다
several 몇몇의

07 The things we learned in kindergarten include "share everything", "play fair", and "say you're sorry when you hurt somebody."

✎

07
kindergarten 유치원
include 포함하다
share 나누다, 함께 하다
fair 규칙에 맞게, 공정하게
hurt 상처를 주다

08 The people you communicate with will feel much more relaxed around you when they feel heard and listened to.

✎

08
communicate with ~와 소통하다
relaxed 편안한, 긴장을 푼

09 You will sometimes find that the person you talk to can convince you that there is really nothing to worry about at all.

✎

09
convince ~을 설득하다
worry about ~에 대해 걱정하다

10 In a commercial society, where having money or wealth is most important, things that can be brought by wealth, such as cars, houses, or fine clothing, are considered status symbols.

✎

10
commercial 상업의
wealth 부, 재산
consider (~을 ~로) 간주하다, 생각하다
status 신분, 지위

11 One of the challenges we face in the world today is that a lot of the information we get about other people and places comes from the advertising and entertainment we see in the media.

✎

11
challenge 도전, 힘든 일
face ~에 직면하다
information 정보
come from ~에서 나오다
advertising 광고
entertainment 오락물

PART 2

절 해석법

UNIT 17 접속사 + S + V

[01 - 14] 다음을 해석하세요.

44

01 When I entered the subway, the thermometer I had with me registered 32℃.

🖉

01
enter ~에 들어가다
subway 지하철
thermometer 온도계
register 기록하다

44

02 We expect that as we tap into new markets, we will see unprecedented growth.

🖉

02
expect 기대하다
tap into 활용[이용]하다
unprecedented 전례가 없는
growth 성장

44

03 If you want to diet, you should consult a physician because it is difficult to select for yourself a proper diet.

🖉

03
diet 다이어트하다
consult 상담하다
physician 의사
select 선택하다, 고르다
proper 적절한

44

04 When his family sets out on a trip to EXPO, his mother says that he doesn't have to join them on the trip because tomorrow they get back home.

🖉

04
set out 출발하다
EXPO 박람회

44

05 The republics of Latvia and Lithuania emphasized their ethnic identities and their own language as they became independent from the Kremlin.

🖉

05
republic 공화국
emphasize 강조하다
ethnic 민족의
identity 정체성
independent 독립한

06 That is, if you can convince yourself that the first draft isn't your best writing and can be made more effective with additional thought and some revision, then it will be easier to get started.

✎

06
convince ~에게 확신시키다
draft 초고, 초안
effective 유효한, 효과적인
additional 추가적인
revision 수정, 개정

07 If you demand that children tell you the truth and then punish them because it is not very satisfying, you teach them to lie to you to protect themselves.

✎

07
demand 요구하다
truth 진실
punish 처벌하다
satisfying 만족한, 충분한
lie 거짓말을 하다
protect 보호하다

08 Since Sam has never been unhappy with his occupation, he cannot understand the attitude of those who have no desire to take up any occupation.

✎

08
since ~하므로
occupation 직업
attitude 태도
desire 욕망, 욕구
take up 차지하다

09 While I cannot promise you that your temporary contract will be extended every time it comes up for review, I can tell you that there do not seem to be any obstacles to further extensions.

✎

09
promise 약속하다
temporary 임시의
contract 계약
extend 연장하다, 늘이다
come up for 고려되다
review 검토
obstacle 장애(물)
extension 연장, 연기

10 In his book *Feminine Faces*, Clovis Chappel wrote that when the Roman city of Pompeii was being excavated, the body of a woman was found mummified by the volcanic ashes of Mount Vesuvius.

✎

10
excavate 발굴하다
mummify 미라로 만들다
volcanic 화산의
ash 재

11

If today's top rock singer released his or her next piece on the Internet, it would not only be like playing in a theater with 20 million seats, but each listener could also transform the music depending upon his or her own personal tastes.

11
release 발표[발매]하다
theater 극장
transform 변형시키다
depending upon ~에 따라
personal 개인의
taste 취향, 기호

12

If they don't provide financial support, you will have to use your emergency fund to cover basic expenses such as food, transport, and accommodation, and there will be less money available for an unexpected situation that necessitates a sudden change of plan.

12
financial 재정적인, 금융의
support 지원, 지지
emergency 비상
fund 자금
cover (무엇을 하기에 충분한 돈을[이]) 대다[되다]
expense 비용, 지출
transport 교통, 운송
accommodation 숙박 시설
available 이용할 수 있는
necessitate 필요로 하다
sudden 갑작스러운

13

There are growing concerns that, as the fourth industrial revolution deepens our individual and collective relationships with technology, it may negatively affect our social skills and ability to empathize.

13
growing 커지는
concern 우려, 관심
the fourth industrial revolution 제4차 산업혁명
deepen 심화하다
individual 개인적인
collective 집단적, 공동의
relationship 관계
negatively 부정적으로
affect ~에게 영향을 미치다
social 사회적인
empathize 공감하다

14

When Steven Erickson and colleagues asked 348 men and 142 women who had been admitted to the hospital for a heart attack about their symptoms and medication, they found that even though the women had more symptoms and were taking more medication, they rated their disease as being no more severe than the men did.

14
colleague 동료
be admitted to the hospital 입원하다
heart attack 심장마비
symptom 증상, 증세
medication 약물 치료
rate 평가하다
severe 심각한, 위중한

복습종이

심슨 구문

🔒 구문분석집 p. 50

[01 - 11] 다음을 해석하세요.

`45`

01 To make their dream come true, they decided not to waste money.

🖉

01
come true 이루어지다, 실현하다
waste 낭비하다

`46`

02 To put a man to death by hanging or electric shock is an extremely cruel form of punishment.

🖉

02
put to death 사형에 처하다
hanging 교수형
electric shock 전기충격
extremely 극히
cruel 잔인한
punishment 형벌

`45`

03 To get some wisdom from superstitions, you need a good education from the intelligent people.

🖉

03
wisdom 지혜, 현명함
superstition 미신
education 교육
intelligent 지성을 갖춘

`45`

04 To win yesterday's competition, he should have spent a lot of time preparing himself but he didn't.

🖉

04
competition 대회, 경쟁
prepare 준비하다

`46`

05 To love someone without any conditions needs bravery and understanding of others and oneself.

🖉

05
bravery 용기
understanding 이해

`46`

06 To understand the true sequence of events by other clues is essential in reading a detective story.

🖉

06
sequence 순서
clue 단서, 실마리
essential 중요한, 필수의
detective story 추리[탐정] 소설

07

To help you celebrate and drink a toast to your success and ours throughout the new year, we have many special dishes on our menus to suit this festive season.

07

celebrate 축하하다, 기념하다
drink a toast to ~을 위해 건배하다
success 성공, 성취
suit ~에 어울리다
festive season 명절, 연말연시

08

Some writers think that to impress their readers, they have to use a lot of long words and try to sound "intellectual."

08

impress ~에게 깊은 인상을 주다
intellectual 지적인

09

For example, to explain why the ancient Egyptians developed a successful civilization, you must look at the geography of Egypt.

09

explain 설명하다
Egyptian 이집트 사람[말]
develop 발전시키다
successful 성공적인, 잘된
civilization 문명
geography 지리, 지형

10

To lower the price of their goods to a reasonable price is the best way to prevent software from being copied illegally and protect the copyright.

10

reasonable 합리적인, 적당한
prevent A from B A가 B하는 것을 막다
copy 복제하다, 복사하다
illegally 불법으로
protect 보호하다
copyright 저작권

11

To entice the most experienced and skilled workers, the company developed a new pay scale for workers that has minimized profits and met all union demands.

11

entice 유치하다, 유인하다
experienced 경험이 많은
skilled 숙련된
pay scale 임금제
minimize 최소로 하다
profit 이윤, 수익
meet (필요·요구 등을) 충족시키다
union 노동조합
demand 요구, 청구

UNIT 19

문장 맨 앞에 RVing/p.p.

🔒 구문분석집 p. 52

[01 - 13] 다음을 해석하세요.

47

01 Looking on at the baseball game, he ran across an old classmate from his high school days.

🖉

48

02 Being wise about the health benefits of sports will ensure a healthy lifestyle.

🖉

47

03 Working with researchers from Chicago University, Bronks has designed its products to meet the special bio-mechanical needs of men and women.

🖉

47

04 While living in over-crowded country, I feel no temptation whatever to drive a car.

🖉

47

05 As surprised by the sudden rainstorm, Sarah quickly ran to find shelter under the nearest tree.

🖉

01
run across ~을 우연히 만나다

02
benefit 이익, 이득
ensure ~을 보장하다

03
researcher 연구원
design 설계[디자인]하다
product 제품, 생산품
bio-mechanical 생체역학의
need 요구, 필요

04
over-crowded 혼잡한
temptation 유혹

05
surprised 놀란
sudden 갑작스러운
rainstorm 폭풍우
quickly 급히
shelter 피난 장소

06

06 Putting an emotion into words and saying it out loud can be a powerful way to express oneself and connect with others on a deeper level.

06
emotion 감정
powerful 강력한
express 표현하다
connect with ~와 친해지다

07

07 Seeing these things later in books will be exciting and enjoyable because they will have real meaning for him.

07
enjoyable 즐거운, 재미있는
real 진정한

08

08 Recognizing the healing power of humor, many hospitals are starting to take laughing matters seriously.

08
recognize 인지하다, 알아보다
healing 치료의, 낫게 하는
matter 일, 문제
seriously 진지하게

09

09 Lifting his hand high over his head, the boy counted off the same number without changing his voice.

09
lift 들어 올리다
count off 숫자를 세다, 번호를 부르다

10

10 Building a meaningful and successful East-West relationship will be possible only with a proper understanding of Asia and Asians.

10
meaningful 의미 있는
successful 성공한
relationship 관계
possible 가능한
proper 올바른, 타당한

11

11 Understanding the movements of heavenly bodies and the relationship between angles and distances, medieval travelers were able to create a system of longitude and latitude.

11
heavenly body 천체
angle 각도
distance 거리
medieval 중세의
longitude 경도
latitude 위도

47

12 Unable to finish college because of a lack of money, he took a job as a playground instructor earning thirty dollars a week.

12
lack 부족, 결핍
instructor 강사
earn 벌다

47

13 Happy with the excellent grades he received, David planned a weekend getaway to the mountains to enjoy some fresh air and nature.

13
excellent 우수한, 훌륭한
grade 성적
receive 받다
getaway 단기 휴가
fresh 신선한

문장 중간에 to RV

🔒 구문분석집 p. 54

[01 - 15] 다음을 해석하세요.

49
01 The objective of some taxes on foreign imports is to protect an industry that produces goods vital to a nation's defense.

01
objective 목적, 목표
tax 세금
foreign 외국의
import 수입
protect 보호하다
industry 산업
defense 방위, 방어

50
02 Social media is a great way to stay in contact with friends and family.

02
stay ~인 채로 유지하다
contact 연락, 접촉

51
03 I was very surprised to receive a phone call from a distant relative whom I hadn't spoken to in years.

03
distant 먼
relative 친척, 친족

52
04 She eventually returned to her native country to escape the pressure, only to find that the media followed her there.

04
eventually 마침내, 결국
return 돌아가다
native country 고국, 모국
escape 벗어나다, 탈출하다
pressure 압박, 압력
follow ~을 따라가다

52
05 Communities are changing their habits in order to protect the environment.

05
community 공동체
habit 습관, 버릇

06

Our purpose is to use governments for the enlargement of our personal freedom, not to be used by them as instruments.

06
purpose 목적, 의도
enlargement 확대, 확장
personal 개인의
freedom 자유
instrument 도구, 기구

07

A common mistake in talking to celebrities is to assume that they don't know much about anything else except their occupations.

07
common 흔한, 공통의
mistake 실수, 잘못
celebrity 유명인, 명사
assume 가정하다
except ~을 제외하고
occupation 직업

08

Many countries now use nuclear power to produce electricity.

08
nuclear power 원자력
electricity 전기

09

The ancient Olympic events were designed to eliminate the weak and glorify the strong.

09
eliminate 탈락시키다, 제거하다
glorify 찬양하다

10

Jim raised over one hundred million dollars to provide relief for the drought victims in Africa.

10
raise 모금하다
relief 구호, 구조
drought 가뭄
victim 피해자, 희생자

11

A group of dedicated volunteers organized a beach clean-up event to raise awareness about environmental conservation.

11
dedicated 헌신적인
volunteer 자원봉사자
organize 조직하다, 구성하다
clean-up 대청소
awareness 인식, 의식

12

Some people, such as engineers and architects, undergo special training exercises to deepen their understanding of design principles and construction techniques.

✏️

12

engineer 엔지니어, 기술자
architect 건축가
undergo 받다, 겪다
training 훈련, 트레이닝
principle 원리, 원칙
construction 건축
technique 기술

13

The capacity to store and distribute information has increased through the use of computers and other devices.

✏️

13

capacity 능력
store 저장하다, 비축하다
distribute 배포하다
device 장치, 설비

14

We need more effective ways to ensure that every citizen can fully exercise the right to secure private information.

✏️

14

effective 효과적인
ensure 보호하다, 보장하다
citizen 시민
fully 충분히, 완전히
secure 보호하다
private information 개인 정보

15

Even with machines, the best way to get data from one to another usually was to physically carry magnetic tapes or punched cards and insert them into other machine.

✏️

15

machine 기계
physically 물리적으로
magnetic 자기의, 자성을 띤
punched card 천공[펀치] 카드
insert (끼워) 넣다, 삽입하다

🔒 구문분석집 p. 58

[01 - 16] 다음을 해석하세요.

`53`

01 Americans have made decisions based on science rather than ideology.

🖉

01
decision 결심, 결의
based on ~에 근거하여
ideology 이념

`54`

02 Color is the most important factor in judging the gem quality of a diamond.

🖉

02
factor 요인, 요소
judge 심사하다, 감정하다
gem 보석
quality 품질

`55`

03 Onlookers just walk by a work of art, letting their eyes record it while their minds are elsewhere.

🖉

03
onlooker 구경꾼, 방관자
record 기록하다
elsewhere 다른 곳으로

`53`

04 The International Monetary Fund(IMF) said that economic trouble affecting Asian countries will begin to better by the first half of 1999.

🖉

04
International Monetary Fund (IMF) 국제통화기금
affect ~에게 영향을 미치다
better 나아지다, 향상되다

`53, 54`

05 In a laboratory conducted at Stanford University, the same changes in plant growth patterns were brought about by touching plants twice a day.

🖉

05
laboratory 실험실, 연구실
conduct 실행하다
growth 성장
bring about ~을 일으키다
twice 두 번

06
Nine-tenths of the woods consumed in the Third World are used for cooking and heating.

✎

06
consume 소비하다
heating 난방(장치)

07
One of the most interesting things ever found under New York's street was a hidden underground tunnel network from the Prohibition era.

✎

07
hidden 숨겨진
Prohibition 금주법 시대

08
Coca-Cola invented in the late 19th century by John Stith Pemberton has been a leading supplier of the world's soft-drink market throughout the 21st century.

✎

08
invent 발명하다, 창안하다
supplier 공급업체
soft-drink 청량음료

09
Good quality North American ice wines, produced in California and British Columbia, have recently come onto the market, making ice wines more affordable.

✎

09
recently 최근
affordable 가격이 저렴한

10
They devoted themselves to hours of unpaid work for the poor and helpless, never minding that few appreciated what they were doing for society.

✎

10
devote 헌신하다
unpaid 무보수의
mind ~에 신경 쓰다
helpless 무력한
appreciate 감사하다

11
Globalization leads more countries to open their markets, allowing them to trade goods and services freely at a lower cost with greater efficiency.

✎

11
globalization 세계화
trade 거래하다, 교역하다
goods and services 상품과 서비스
freely 자유로이, 맘대로
cost 비용, 가격
efficiency 효율, 능률

12 Aggression among animal populations can be significantly decreased only by relocating the competitive species.

✎

12
aggression 공격성
population 개체군, 개체 수
significantly 크게, 상당히
decrease 감소하다, 축소하다
relocate 재배치하다
competitive 경쟁적인
species 종

13 Water as a universal solvent makes all life possible by providing essential minerals and nutrients needed to grow and stay healthy.

✎

13
universal 보편적인, 일반적인
solvent 용매
mineral 미네랄
nutrient 영양소

14 An infomercial is a television commercial lasting approximately thirty minutes and used to sell a product by convincing viewers that they must have the product.

✎

14
infomercial 인포머셜(해설형 광고)
television commercial TV 광고
last 지속하다
approximately 약, 거의
sell 판매하다
convince 설득하다
viewer 시청자

15 There is no basis for believing that technology will not cause new and unanticipated problems while solving the problems that it previously produced.

✎

15
basis 근거, 기초
unanticipated 예상하지 못한
solve 해결하다
previously 이전에

16 While the first step in alleviating poverty in the developing world is providing adequate food and shelter, a long-term solution to the problem must focus on other issues.

✎

16
alleviate 완화하다
poverty 빈곤, 가난
adequate 적절한, 적당한
solution 해결책, 해답
focus on 초점을 맞추다
issue 문제, 쟁점

MEMO

4

그 밖의 핵심 구문

복습종이

심슨 구문

🔒 구문분석집 p. 62

[01 - 15] 다음을 해석하세요.

56
01 It is dangerous to go out too late at night.
✎

01
dangerous 위험한

56
02 It is necessary that you should see a doctor right now.
✎

02
necessary 필요한

57
03 He thinks it reasonable for young people to wear what they like.
✎

03
reasonable 합리적인, 타당한, 이성적인
wear 입다

57
04 I think it certain that our team will win the game.
✎

04
certain 확실한, 어떤

56
05 It is also important for the journalist to remember that his duty is to serve his readers.
✎

05
journalist 언론인
remember 기억하다
duty 의무, 본분
serve ~을 위해 일하다

56
06 In Britain and some other European countries, it was the custom for women to have the right to propose marriage to the men of their choice.
✎

06
custom 관습, 풍습
propose marriage to ~에게 청혼하다
choice 선택

07 To bring about an increase in exports, it is important for us to sell commodities of excellent quality and a low price.

🖉

07
bring about 가져오다, 초래하다
increase 증가, 인상
export 수출
commodity 상품, 일용품
excellent 우수한, 뛰어난
quality 품질
low 낮은
price 가격

08 It is true that one of the chief goals in child-raising in the United States is to develop a sense of independence in the child.

🖉

08
chief 주요한, 주된
goal 목표, 목적
child-raising 자녀 양육
sense of independence 독립심

09 It is often believed that the function of school is to produce knowledgeable people.

🖉

09
function 기능, 작용
knowledgeable 지식이 있는

10 It is often said that the best way to learn a foreign language is to go to a country where it is spoken.

🖉

10
foreign language 외국어

11 It is my great pleasure to inform you that your sons and daughters have completed all the academic requirements over the last three years of study at Hutt High School.

🖉

11
pleasure 기쁨, 즐거움
inform ~에게 알리다, 통지하다
complete 완성하다, 달성하다
academic 학업의, 학교의
requirement 요건, 필요조건

12 In some cultures, people think it wrong to share their feelings and worries with others.

🖉

12
wrong 잘못된, 틀린
share 공유하다
feeling 감정, 기분
worry 걱정, 근심

13

13 She found it difficult to understand the complicated instructions without any guidance or support from others.

complicated 복잡한, 까다로운
instruction 제품의 사용 설명서, 지시, 교육
guidance 지도, 안내
support 지원, 지지, 후원

14

14 The Internet has made it possible for an enormous amount of information to be accessible from anywhere in the world.

enormous 엄청난, 거대한
accessible 접근할 수 있는

15

15 I find it funny that my cat insists on sleeping on my laptop when I'm trying to work.

insist on 고집을 부리다

🔒 구문분석집 p. 66

[01 - 12] 다음을 해석하세요.

58

01 He has been asking questions and listening to people's complaints about city government.

✎

01
complaint 불만, 불평

58

02 Rituals like looking at your watch, reaching for a car key, and untying shoes are seldom forgotten.

✎

02
ritual 의식, 절차, (개인의) 습관적 행위
untie 풀다, 끄르다
seldom 좀처럼 ~ 않는

58

03 In spite of their continued efforts, factories and cars are still producing too much dirty smoke and putting too many chemicals into the air.

✎

03
in spite of ~불구하고
continued 지속적인
effort 노력, 수고
factory 공장
smoke 매연, 연기
chemicals 화학물질

58

04 It may even be necessary to visit distant towns and villages to collect information from the people who live there.

✎

04
distant 멀리 떨어진, 먼
village 마을
collect 수집하다, 모으다

58

05 Getting a good night's sleep before the test and eating a nutritious breakfast will enhance your alertness and help you feel relaxed.

✎

05
nutritious 영양가 많은
enhance 향상하다, 늘리다
alertness 기민
relaxed 긴장을 푼, 편한

PART 4

그밖의 핵심 구문

06

Hanging by their teeth, swinging with one arm, and turning over in the air are just a few of the acts that circus stars do high over head.

06
hang by ~으로 매달다
swing 그네를 타다
turn over 몸[자세]을 뒤집다

07

The balls were first made of grass or leaves held together by strings, and later of pieces of animal skin sewn together and stuffed with feathers or hay.

07
hold together 결합하다
string 끈, 줄
skin 가죽
stuff A with B A를 B로 채우다
feather 깃털
hay 건초

08

Our reliable construction team plans the design you need, obtains local authority approval, and gets our extension built with a guarantee of satisfaction.

08
reliable 신뢰할 수 있는
construction 건설, 건축
obtain 얻다, 획득하다
authority 기관, 당국
approval 승인, 허가
extension 확장, 증축
guarantee 보증
satisfaction 만족(감)

09

Every advance in human understanding since then has been made by brave individuals daring to step into the unknown darkness and to break free from accepted ways of thinking.

09
advance 진보, 향상
brave 용감한
individual 개인
unknown 알려지지 않은
darkness 어둠, 암흑
break free from ~에서 벗어나다, 자유로워지다
accepted 일반적으로 인정된

10

We learn formal skills like learning a foreign language and doing a proof in physics, not by reading a textbook and understanding the abstract principles, but by actually solving problems in those fields.

10
formal 형식의
skill 기술
proof 증명, 증거
physics 물리학
textbook 교과서
abstract 추상적인
principle 원리, 원칙
field 분야

58

11 A suitable insurance policy should provide coverage for medical expenses arising from illness or accident prior to or during their vacation, loss of vacation money, and cancellation of the holiday.

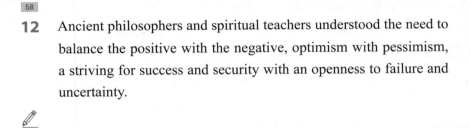

58

12 Ancient philosophers and spiritual teachers understood the need to balance the positive with the negative, optimism with pessimism, a striving for success and security with an openness to failure and uncertainty.

11

suitable 적절한
insurance 보험
policy 정책, 방침
coverage 보장 범위
medical 의학의
expense 지출, 비용
arise from ~에서 발생하다
accident 사고
prior to ~에 앞서

12

philosopher 철학자
spiritual 영적인, 정신의
positive 긍정적인
negative 부정적인
optimism 낙관주의
pessimism 비관주의
striving 노력, 분투
security 안전
failure 실패
uncertainty 불안정

PART 4

그 밖의 핵심 구문

🔒 구문분석집 p. 68

[01 - 12] 다음을 해석하세요.

`59`
01 Feeling pure and complete sorrow is as impossible as feeling pure and complete joy.

✏️

01
pure 순수한
complete 완전한
sorrow 슬픔
impossible 불가능한

`60`
02 The bigger the expectation is, the smaller the satisfaction is.

✏️

02
expectation 기대
satisfaction 만족

`59`
03 Visiting a farm is far more educational than looking at a book about a farm, where your child can pat a cow, hear ducks quack, and smell hay.

✏️

03
educational 교육적인
pat 쓰다듬다
quack 꽥꽥 우는 소리

`59`
04 Processing a TV message is much more like the all-at-once processing of the ear than the linear processing of the eye reading a printed page.

✏️

04
process 처리하다
all-at-once 일괄적, 모두 함께[동시에]
linear 선형의, 직선 모양의

`59`
05 A person who feels bad with reasonable regularity will enjoy the occasional period of feeling good far more than somebody who feels good so often that he is bored by it.

✏️

05
regularity 규칙적임
occasional 때때로의, 임시의

06 Rosberg observed that color advertisements in the trade publication *Industrial Marketing* produced more attention than black and white advertisements.

06
observe 말하다, 진술하다
advertisement 광고
publication 간행(물), 출판(물)
attention 관심, 주의

07 According to research from the University of Chicago, individuals without strong bonds of friendship, family, or community get colds at four times the rate of people who have such bonds.

07
according to ~에 따르면
bond 유대(감), 결속
friendship 우정

08 As we'll see, people who devote immense amount of time to political news can actually be more misinformed and less reasonable than those of us who spend far less time following politics.

08
devote (시간·노력 등을) 바치다
immense 막대한
political 정치의
misinformed 잘못된 정보를 받고 있는
politics 정치(학)

09 Managers who want people to take a more team-based approach with their people, for example, will almost certainly get better results by taking a more team-based approach themselves rather than just by making a speech on teamwork.

09
approach 접근
result 결과, 성과

10 The more we try to anticipate these problems, the better we can control them.

10
anticipate 예측하다, 예상하다
control 통제하다

PART 4

그 밖의 핵심 구문

11 The harder you work, the more likely you are to get good grades, and the brighter your future will be.

12 The more people there are in a conversation, the less well you know them, and the more status differences among them, the more a conversation is like public speaking or report-talk.

11

grade 성적, 학점

12

conversation 대화
status (사회적) 지위
difference 차이, 다름

기타 구문/기호의 쓰임새

🔒 구문분석집 p. 71

[01 - 15] 다음을 해석하세요.

61

01 The old man sat looking out the window, with his wife sewing beside him.

01

sew 바느질하다

61

02 With much less emphasis placed on words, many Asian cultures rely heavily on nonverbal cues and social context to derive meaning.

02

emphasis 강조
place 놓다, 두다
rely on ~에 의지하다
heavily 크게, 몹시
nonverbal 비언어적인
cue 신호, 단서
context 맥락, 전후 관계, 문맥
derive 끌어내다

61

03 With face-to-face conversations crowded out by online interactions, the richness of real-life interactions may be lost.

03

face-to-face 대면하는, 마주 보는
crowd out 밀어내다, 몰아내다
interaction 상호 작용
richness 풍부, 부유
real-life 현실의

62

04 Many people believe that all they have to do to relieve an acute migraine headache is to take pain-killing drugs.

04

relieve 완화하다, 경감하다, 덜다
acute 급성의
migraine 편두통
pain-killing 통증[고통]을 죽이는
drug 약

62

05 Climate change is making it more difficult for plant-eating animals to locate food.

05

plant-eating 식물을 먹는
locate 찾아내다, 위치를 찾다

06

62

Sun-dried fruits, like apricots and raisins, make delicious and healthy snacks for quick energy boosts.

✎

06
sun-dried 햇볕에 말린
apricot 살구
raisin 건포도
delicious 맛있는
boost 증가

07

62

By understanding our health-related motivations, we gain insights into barriers that keep us from enjoying better health as we age.

✎

07
motivation 동기
gain 얻다, 획득하다
insight 통찰(력)
barrier 장벽

08

63

The bookstore specializes in three subjects: art, architecture, and graphic design.

✎

08
specialize 전문으로 한다
subject 주제
architecture 건축

09

63

Some firms sell cigarettes; others sell products that help you quit smoking.

✎

09
cigarette 담배
quit smoking 금연하다

10

63

Heavy snow continues to fall at the airport; consequently, all flights have been canceled.

✎

10
consequently 그 결과
flight 항공편
cancel 취소하다

11

63

Even the simplest tasks — washing, dressing, and going to work — were nearly impossible after I broke my leg.

✎

11
task 일
nearly 거의, 대략
impossible 불가능한

12 The digital revolution means that sooner or later students and adults are going to need an entirely new set of skills: how to get information, where to find it, and how to use it.

🖉

12
revolution 혁명, 변혁
entirely 완전히

13 A woman may save her household money to carpet her bedrooms; her neighbor may save hers to buy a second car.

🖉

13
save 절약[저축]하다
household 가계의, 가족[가정]의

14 By most estimates, more than 500 million people — roughly one out of every nine — suffer from serious malnutrition today, compared with 100 million to 200 million — one out of every 14 to 25 people in the 1950's.

🖉

14
estimate 추산, 견적
roughly 대략
suffer from ~을 겪다
malnutrition 영양실조
compared with ~과 비교하여, ~와 비교해서

15 Some heroes shine in the face of great adversity, performing amazing deeds in difficult situations; other heroes do their work quietly, unnoticed by most of us, but making a difference in the lives of other people.

🖉

15
adversity 역경, 불행
perform 수행하다, 실행하다
deed 행동, 행위
unnoticed 주목되지 않은

PART 4

그밖의 핵심 구문

REVIEW
TEST

복습종이

심슨 구문

REVIEW TEST

🔒 구문분석집 p. 84

[01 - 31] 다음을 해석하세요.

01 Of all the housework she did, what she hated most was to wash the dishes.

✎

02 Thunderstorms are made when the summer air near the ground is hot but the air a few miles up is freezing cold.

✎

03 If you have a big job with lots of paper work, we have a little idea that might help you get through it more efficiently.

✎

04 They also include subconscious thought that you were not even aware you were thinking until you sat down to write.

✎

05 When you are going on a hike or a summer vacation, try to stay away from places that are full of either poison ivy or poison oak.

✎

06 One of the first things that people studying English learn is that the game called football is called soccer in North America.

✎

07 We often hear stories of ordinary people who, if education had focused on creativity, could have become great artists or scientists.

🖉

08 A common belief is that if we find someone who likes to do the same thing we do, then we will get along and we will be happy.

🖉

09 When a co-worker announced one morning that he and his wife were expecting their first child, we all gathered around to congratulate him.

🖉

10 They must accept the criticism of others but be suspicious of it, and they must accept the praise of others but be even more suspicious of it.

🖉

11 I have widened my horizons to include many delightful people whom I might have never known if I had maintained my original judgement.

🖉

12 Adding substances to foods to give them color, enhance their flavor, or interrupt the monotony of eating the same foods day after day is not new.

🖉

13 Those seeking a job — the young and the unskilled — realized that the best way to get hired is to acquire some experience from volunteer work.

14 Biologists studying sleep have concluded that it makes little difference whether a person habitually sleeps during the day or during the night.

15 I'm still walking on a great big cloud, so when I meet you at the station, don't be surprised if you can't see me for the rays of happiness surrounding me.

16 Air traffic controllers report that the long stretches of doing relatively little are at least as stressful as the time when they are handling many aircraft in the sky.

17 For one thing, you might have a job, but unless it is very well-paid, you will not be able to afford many things because living in a city is often very expensive.

18 Situated at an elevation of 1,350 m, the city of Kathmandu, which looks out on the sparkling Himalayas, enjoys a warm climate year-round that makes living here pleasant.

19 Some universities remain silent on the important issues of the day, justifying their silence on the grounds that universities are neutral and should not become involved.

✏️

20 Instead of treating different patients that display similar symptoms with the same drugs, doctors should identify root causes of disease to come up with a personalized treatment.

✏️

21 Our incredible growth rate leads to a continuous recruitment of ambitious programmer analysts who have the desire to make a significant contribution to an expanding company.

✏️

22 If the painting you looked at was a seascape, you may have liked it because the dark colors and enormous waves reminded you of the wonderful memories you had in your hometown.

✏️

23 Many creatures use *phosphorescence at night, and as you move through the water, you will cause plankton to release tiny pulses of light, leaving beautiful glowing wakes trailing behind you.

✏️

24 Nowadays, living in an over-crowded country where traffic is continuously on the increase, and where driving is controlled by a great many rules and regulations, I feel no temptation to drive a car.

✏️

25 The manufacturers who produce art reproductions and the consumers who purchase and display them give value to the work of art by making it available to many people as an item of popular culture.

🖊

26 Also, attending a live performance may let you catch many subtle details that are hidden from TV viewers at home, like a faint smile on a performer's face. That smile may add a whole new meaning to the performance!

🖊

27 In pointing out the misconceptions that the public has about a scientist's life, the speaker stated that the popular picture of the dedicated scientist spending long hours in peaceful contemplation is true but misleading.

🖊

28 People who make friends with many different people before they get married seem to have a variety of friends during their adult life, relate to other people in more positive ways, and have a more lasting relationship in their marriage.

🖊

29 No matter where you go, no matter who your ancestors were, what school or college you have attended, or who helps you, your best opportunity is in you. The help you get from others is something outside of you, while it is what you are, what you do, that counts.

🖊

30 One researcher conducted in-depth interviews with people who were imprisoned for violent behavior. The interviews revealed that children who are frequently spanked or threatened with violence are at very high risk of learning that violence is a way to solve problems, get what they want, or protect themselves from a perceived threat.

🖉

31 A medical study found that children aged six to eleven who had been enrolled at large daycare centers as toddlers had about one-third as many colds as children who had stayed home as toddlers. Dr. Thomas Ball, one of the participants in the study, says that when children have colds as toddlers, their immune systems are learning from these experiences, and this learning will come back to protect children later in life.

🖉

Staff

Writer	심우철
Director	강다비다
Researcher	정규리 / 한선영 / 장은영 / 김도현
Design	강현구
Manufacture	김승훈
Marketing	윤대규 / 한은지 / 유경철

발행일: 2024년 7월 18일 (개정 1판)

내용문의: http://cafe.naver.com/shimson2000